ANNIE

— AND THE —

GIGOLO'S

Romantic Online
Lurking Evil,
Lust and Greed takes,
Love gives

HERB KLINGELE

BALBOA.PRESS

A DIVISION OF HAY HOUSE

Balboa Press books may be ordered through booksellers or by contacting:

Balboa Press
A Division of Hay House
1663 Liberty Drive
Bloomington, IN 47403
www.balboapress.com
844-682-1282

Because of the dynamic nature of the Internet, any web addresses or links contained in this book may have changed since publication and may no longer be valid. The views expressed in this work are solely those of the author and do not necessarily reflect the views of the publisher, and the publisher hereby disclaims any responsibility for them.

The author of this book does not dispense medical advice or prescribe the use of any technique as a form of treatment for physical, emotional, or medical problems without the advice of a physician, either directly or indirectly. The intent of the author is only to offer information of a general nature to help you in your quest for emotional and spiritual well-being. In the event you use any of the information in this book for yourself, which is your constitutional right, the author and the publisher assume no responsibility for your actions.

Any people depicted in stock imagery provided by Getty Images are models, and such images are being used for illustrative purposes only.
Certain stock imagery © Getty Images.

Print information available on the last page.

ISBN: 978-1-9822-6243-3 (sc)
ISBN: 978-1-9822-6242-6 (e)

Balboa Press rev. date: 02/04/2021

CONTENTS

DEDICATION

JANESSA IS A SWEETHEART; WITH loving-kindness, consideration, and a real loving heart for others. Thomas has researched so many online dating scams, like the picture Annie was using.

This beautiful model from Brazil, who 86 romance scammers, is using her photos. Thank you, Janessa, for the telephone call and the time you spent with Thomas.

FOREWORD

A WARNING TO ONLINE ROMANTIC scammers, God is watching. One million years from now, your soul will be in one of two places, heaven or hell. And the choices made during this life's trials and tribulations will determine your destiny for eternity. Matthew 7; 13. *Enter ye in at the strait gate: for comprehensive is the gate, and broad is the way, that leadeth to destruction, and many there be which go in there at:*

PREFACE

TO TEST THE SPIRIT OF THE TRUTH;

THE UNBELIEVERS OF THE TRUTH do not want examination. Suppose you criticize the unbelievers of fact if you endeavored to contend for the truth. And you expose their error, they will turn it around and condemn you as a sinner. If this is the Holy Spirit's actual work, they would be inviting all the scrutiny they could get if they were honest and trustworthy. They would want the affirmation and authentication if they were genuine?

Being deceitful and fraudulent in the Errors of their ways. You are the one standing in their way of the truth in the Bible and the teachings of Jesus. For them to succeed, they have to turn iniquity into a transgression against Christ. Sound doctrine proves that they do not survive.

INTRODUCTION

"ANNIE AND THE GIGOLO'S." IN this manuscript, there is a love between Annie through an online Christian dating service of how most couples meet. As a result, Annie falls in love with a gentleman, and this goes on and on.

Through Annie's pictures and all of her lies, deceit, and fraudulent ways, you will find, for the most part, if you're looking at the pictures. Possibly you are not looking at the picture you think you're looking at, and you tend to fall in love because of the words this fraudulent lady Annie keeps promising love sending more pictures. And behind Annie's deceitful dark lurching ways is a gigolo. This gigolo controls ladies and supposedly protect them.

However, we have found out through experience these gigolos are nothing but cowards and hide behind these ladies taking Annie's money as fast as the online sucker man who keeps providing with false promises.

A side note for published authors; they will take an autobiography of a published author to skim through it. And Annie will contact the author and start a romantic interlude and slowly mention things that they both have in common, which mystifies the author as miraculous. And before you know it, the author is hooked. And the only reason Annie knows these things is that she is familiar with reading his book.

It so looks like Thomas's' good friend Annie is going to do 12 years minimum. She has played in scamming Thomas. She may be going away where they will have to pipe her sunshine down, and she is going to be underground so far. Romantic scammers think they're adorable. They are all in for a big surprise.

Please have patience, and Thomas feels Ginette must call the authorities and tell them about Annie having Ginette's passport with Ginette's signature on it. Thomas also has every receipt of every iPhone and computer mailed to Thomas's home and had them forwarded to New York at Annie's request.

Everything, and they send in a government bookkeeper to organize all the fraudulent activities she has done, thinking she is getting away with scamming. At the appropriate agencies' request, Thomas also sent Annie a fake military identification card that's federal. The number is not Thomas's no. is directly associated with the proper authorities in Canada. They are trying to take down these scammers.

Annie asked for Thomas's driver's license if Thomas would scan it and send it to her, and it is affiliated with the proper authorities in Canada. So whoever uses Thomas's driver's license is going. Annie's thinking is a little impaired; Annie could not use any of Thomas's IDs. She would have to have a gigolo or a man, her bed partner.

Annie even asked for Thomas's Social Security number. Thomas gave her an agent's card, and whoever uses that to where the sodomites live. Thomas would never give out his credentials and keep in mind Ginette your signature on a fake passport with your signature; Thomas suggests not hesitate to call the authorities if Ginette does not, maybe liable for however they use it, just a thought.

This goes on for quite some time between Thomas and Annie. Thomas has a suspicion because of the lies that he lets go because he has fallen in love with Annie. And she keeps dangling the carrot in front of him even though Thomas knows he is being taken advantage of with the thoughts that possibly one day they will get together and get married. How Thomas found out was through a publishing agent from the Philippines that noticed that this lady Annie was a phony, which led Thomas to investigate. Thomas was in total disbelief. Sure enough, the more research, more Thomas found out about all the lies and she was telling him. She was on numerous dating sites and even made pornography movies and model for pornography films and shots of pictures.

CHAPTER 1

LUST FOR WORLDLY POSSESSIONS
TO FIND HAPPINESS

THE GREED AND THE LOVE of money lust for worldly possessions to find happiness and think they are no happiness and love. What they forget is, God is watching. God will judge them, by their thoughts, by their words, what they do, and what they fail to do.

And one thing Annie never did was share her life with Thomas. Thomas emptied his soul to her, and she gave nothing in return. Not even a postcard, and when Thomas found out the pictures, Annie was not. As Thomas confronted Annie, she denied it and lied and lied and made up some big excuse and even got angry that Thomas would even insinuate such an accusation. And then she stopped sending pictures at all. All she was interested in was using Thomas's address to have computers, and iPhone sent to Thomas. And Thomas would send them on to an address in New York City, and from there, they would be mailed to Annie and her gigolo. More than likely, in Africa where they could get big money for these items. Thomas noticed they were using other Social Security numbers for the purchase and delivered to Thomas's home.

Thomas lives alone in what used to be a bachelor pad, and the promises of Annie to come and live with Thomas found Thomas remodeling this three bedrooms two bath shack into a beautiful home. Thomas always looks at the right side of things and looks at the good stuff and Thomas has brought into his life. Thomas now has that beautifully remodeled home he has turned his life around; as far as looking at pornography, Thomas finds it repulsive. And he has dove headfirst into theology and studying the Bible almost 24 hours a day. Devoting his life to God and service as you will keep reading the love Thomas as for God through prayers, Faith, and love for God through Jesus Christ our Lord's name in the Holy Spirit that moves throughout the earth answering prayers.

Annie calls Thomas once in a while as Thomas look at the call back number, and it is her. As soon as Thomas picks up the telephone, she hangs up. Thomas is not sure what that is all about, and he will not talk to her again, and the emails have abruptly stopped. Although Thomas thanks Annie for getting him started journaling and contacting publishers and began writing books. Annie made a note, extensively long emails to Thomas, that Thomas has quite an education to pass on to others scammed romantically and fraudulently by these ladies. Thomas doing research, found out that in Canada, romantic scammers get six years in prison and possibly up to 12 years in prison. For instance, in the United States is like a slap on the hand the maximum they can get is two years and possibly a fine. Not Canada.

So you men out there, be careful; you can fall in love very quickly with a picture and even get telephone calls from these ladies, and they will be so convincing that you are just the man for them. Fortunately for Thomas, it did not cost a lot of money. Thomas only sent computers and iPhones that Annie had sent to Thomas's house. God only knows, and Thomas could mail them to New York as Annie would even send Thomas the shipping label. Simply amazing.

CHAPTER 2

THOMAS SONG;
THE LUST AND GREED OF A GIRL NAMED ANNIE AND HER GIGOLO'S

FOR YOU, MY FRIEND. WHAT if your friend was gone tomorrow and you never told them how you felt? What if you never again heard their voice, never saw their face, or felt the warm embrace? I want to say that you are very special to me, and you made a difference in my life. I care for you.

I've been cheated, I've been mistreated, have been taken advantage of, I've been kicked down, when will I be loved. Well, it's time for a new lady, and it's time for mine. It always breaks my heart and happens all the time. I've been fraudulently lied to; when will I be loved. When I find a new lady through the Grace of God patiently, I wait not to be lied to, not to be put down, not to be mistreated or cheated—burning hurting memories.

Exodus 34: 7. *Keeping mercy for thousands, forgiving iniquity and transgression and sin, and that will by no means clear the guilty; visiting the fathers' iniquity upon the children, and upon the children's children, unto the third and to the fourth generation.*

Ephesians 5; 6-8. *Let no man deceive you with vain words, for because of these things comes the wrath of God upon the children of disobedience. Be not you, therefore, partakers with them. For you were sometimes darkness, but now are you light in the Lord; walk as children of light.*

Peace will begin to let it begin with me. Let me bring help for my soul the peace allows it to start with me to the Holy Spirit. My life, the good of my life, is all I control that the piece of my soul begins with me. Let me tell which you been teaching me; you been bringing colors around my blue. I have discovered dreams in the life I have found. Trees were falling from the trees, and the moon with its falling light in the breeze coming through the trees. The dreams I discover in my life are the dreams that I dream, and a miraculous wonder of these dreams keeps coming. 1 Peter 2; 24. Who his self-bare our sins in His own body on the tree, that we, being dead to sins, should live unto righteousness: by whose stripes ye were healed.

You should have seen me travel that far. What is new you would make it, and I'll bet your dad he's proud of you now. She seems to have gone to California; she loves wearing those flowery shirts. And I can say with my mouth turned down someone misses you. Friend, you are if I had a golden star, I would pin it on you. They all had a friend of mine until you came along. You were there before I needed you, and you already knew. And when I had nothing, you came through, and the others did not care. The kind of friend you can never scare away, and you said you would always stay.

A special friend, and here you are before I needed you. You know that I needed a friend, a special friend, and here you are.1Corinthians 6:9 – 11. Or do you not know that the unrighteous will not inherit the kingdom of God? Do not be deceived: neither the sexually immoral, idolaters, nor adulterers, nor men who practice homosexuality, nor thieves, nor the greedy, nor drunkards, nor revilers, nor swindlers will inherit the kingdom of God. And such were some of you. But you were washed, you were sanctified, you were justified in the name of the Lord Jesus Christ and by the Spirit of our God.

I cannot give my girl Annie diamonds or pearls, although I do have the sun in the moonlight. I've got no mansion, I have no yacht, but I'm happy with what I got. I have the sun in the morning and the moon at night in the gracious Spirit that gives me life. The Angels cried because they knew what was to come, and the tears of the Angels were to go because they knew that God above had sent his Son. And tender hearts were soon to come that were meant to be, and the Angels gathered round.

James 3; 8. *But the tongue can no man tame; it is an unruly evil, full of deadly poison.*

It would help if you did not worry about me because I'm all right. I don't care what you say anymore because this is my life. Go ahead with your own life and leave me alone. Don't get me wrong, and I stood alone in your life of friends you could not dream of your home. We were like a wildfire burning out of control. And she told me it would never and but I wish I knew now what I knew then. Once again, I found myself running for shelter again against the wind. Psalms 17; 9. *From the wicked that oppress me, from my deadly enemies, who compass me about.*

We are two ways away from home, and she saw him, and she kept running away and against the wind. From the start, I knew in my heart this would not be meant to be; although I Trying to shine the light to let her see the way and she never shows the morning, she walked in the dark, and we separated and came apart. Do not even try to understand; I just tried to find a place and take a stand. And take it easy. John 8; 24. *Therefore, I said that ye should die in your sins: for if ye believe not that I am he, ye shall die in your sins.*

My dreamboat Annie you are just a ship of dreams. One way or another, Weatherby next week next month years from now we will meet. I had to go now, and you did not have to see me cry because of the lies and the deceit in the fraudulent dual lifestyle a materialistic gigolo's. They always have, and I never with nothing but a fool. Although the Holy Spirit, through the Grace of God, my Faith in my prayers have brought me a life you could have only dreamed. 1 John 1; 6-10. If we say that we have fellowship with God and walk in darkness, we lie and do not the truth. But if we walk in the light, as God is in the light, we have fellowship one with another, and the blood of Jesus Christ, his Son, cleanses us from all sin. If we say that we have no sin, we deceive ourselves, and the truth is not in us. If we confess our sins, he is faithful and forgives us our sins and cleanse us from all unrighteousness.

If we say that we have not sinned, we make God a liar, and the Lord's word is not in us.

Thomas's so-called good friend Annie has never confessed or forsaken them, so therefore she can never be saved from the way she feels she has. When we confess our sins and leave our sins, never to do them again is only the time God will forgive us. If we continue on our ways of evil, we will be judged accordingly. Leviticus 26; 18. *And if ye will not yet for all this hearken unto me, then I will punish you seven times more for your sins.*

You never have opened your heart or have been honest or truthful, always taken advantage of the gigolo's and having the so-called last laugh. Prayer and love and forgiveness, and I want to thank you for giving me what you have provided even though you do not see these gifts have come to me through the Grace of God, my unshakeable Faith, my prayers, and my love for God. John 8; 44. *Ye are of your father, the devil, and the lusts of your father ye will do. From the beginning, he was a murderer and abode not in the truth because there is no truth in him. When he speaketh a lie, he speaketh of his own: for he is a liar and the father of it.*

I had to try for that one lost sheep and shine the light and gave everything I had. And thank God for bringing us together in the most miraculous way for the reason there is something better down the road for each of us. So you see, we had to come together with our similarities. It was a time we found each other, and we would never let each other go. We used to say there was no way this love would ever separate through the Grace of God. What we did not realize is that there is something better for each of us down the road. Romans 3; 4. *God forbid: yea, let God be true, but every man a liar; as it is written, That thou mightest be justified in thy sayings, and mightest overcome when thou art judged.*

My calling through spiritual discernment not-for-profit or prestige to help many hundreds of thousands of others get to the gates of heaven, the Golden Road, the one less traveled. And God shines his life before

Thomas and his light, and I know my way. Thomas has no regrets and no resentments, only love and forgiveness. Matthew 7:13, *Enter ye in at the strait gate: for wide is the gate, and broad is the way, that leadeth to destruction, and many there be which go in there at.*

You can only enter heaven through the "strait gate," because strait is the gate, and narrow is the way, which leadeth unto life, and few there be that find it.

The STRAIT GATE and NARROW...WAY is a total commitment to Jesus Christ. It is not just saying, Lord, Lord. It is not just saying you have accepted Jesus as your Savior. Many name the name of Jesus, but they perish. The STRAIT GATE and NARROW...WAY is: BE YE DOERS OF THE WORD, AND NOT HEARERS ONLY, DECEIVING YOUR SELVES.

I feel in my heart that we will most certainly miss each other we have a memory to cherish that no matter the wedge that came between us, the love Will never separate, and we will always miss each other. It was the most beautiful dream in the most miraculous gift God could have given. A man can cry and put back in the fire to the Grace of God to this gold. One day we will see each other, and we will say my it's been a long time. How am I doing? Although our mothers know our fathers know that we always have and we always will love within our hearts. And there'll be a time, if not already, as she doesn't cry anymore. Ezekiel 16; 15. *But thou didst trust in thine own beauty, and playedst the harlot because of thy renown, and poured out thy fornications on every one that passed by; his it was.*

Walking on eggshells, I wanted to believe although it was a bleeding love and as graciously as it seems like sometimes you are sitting right next to me and I was sitting right next to you. Our love bled in hurt, and the prayers I love God, I love the prayers. I often think of the life I lived and wonder why I'm not dead. My calling through the Grace of God was the love that I cried for you. 1 Corinthian's 6; 18 – 20. *Flee sexual immorality. [Now this is to the Corinthian church, and they were full of sexual problems. So, he was going to address it.] Every sin that a man does is outside the body, but he commits sexual immorality sins against his own body. Or do you not know that your body is the temple of the Holy Spirit who is in you, whom you have from God, and you are not your own? [You don't own your own body.] For you were bought at a price [Who owns it?]; therefore, glorify God in your body and in your Spirit, which is God's.*

I did it for you all of my life, and here I am in everything I used to do. Although I felt like the great imposter when you never felt in my heart that you stuck with me, it was like you were that girl from the North country chasing that financial security will never come. However, I cannot help but wonder how you are doing. That girl from the North country was once mine, and peace will go, although I cannot help but wonder where and why and what you have done? Proverbs 6; 16 – 20. *There are six things that the Lord hates, seven that are an abomination to him: haughty eyes, a lying tongue, and hands that shed innocent blood, a heart that devises wicked plans, feet that make haste to run to evil, a false witness who breathes out lies, and one who sows discord among brothers.*

You're the hero on my mind from time to time, although you are going to make me lonesome and only because I fell in love with you. And I know you will never follow me. I want you to be happy and free; you were my destiny, and you may be right; the story is in your eyes the mirrors of the soul is the vision of love, and we will never be born to lose; it's just your cheating heart. For life, I could never provide or care for you, although you had light up my life, and you were my all and all, and that was the word God spake.

Myself my calling, I will die to live eternally and not be lost in flames. How could an angel break my heart, and sometimes I wonder why? And this life is the speed of light Anna Valentine that will never be near only one day when my little girl smiles.

There is nothing like the real deal, and I would not say these words if I didn't care. I'm not a magic man; I do not have any magic answers. I only have the truth in the Faith in trying to do the next right thing growing along spiritual lines singing a song for you. I've been everywhere, and I had the rhythm with the devil, and you were like that secret love I just Trying to show the light. I will survive as yourself, and I will always have a song for you. Matthew 13.; [44]Jesus said. Again, the kingdom of heaven is like unto treasure hid in a field; the which when a man has found, he hideth, and for joy thereof goes and sells all that he has, and buys that field. [45]Again, the kingdom of heaven is like unto a merchant man, seeking goodly pearls. [46]Who, when he has found one pearl of great price, went and sold all that he had, and bought it.

Because the Spirit carries on, and I have experienced the cold shot. Don't get me wrong, and I would not have changed one moment; no regrets will always have a love and forgiveness for you. And you taught me well to rid the disease of broken stones of worldly lust.

Proverbs 6; *23For the commandment is a lamp, and the law is the light; the reproof of instruction are the way of life. 24To keep you from the evil woman, from the flattery of the tongue and of a strange woman. 25For utilizing a whorish woman, man is brought to a piece of bread; and the adulterous will hunt for the precious life. 27Can a man take fire in his bosom, and his close not be burned? 20Can one go upon hot coals, and his feet not be burned?*

I will never be a fallen angel, especially remembering your pictures in how you look even if I do not have anybody. I have the Holy Spirit. I keep God first in Jesus Christ, our Lord, through my Faith, prayers, and love for God. I will travel one day across the universe, possibly obscured by clouds and passed by collapsing the light into the earth to stay awake and not to be forever down and never to be a fallen angel. 2 Peter 2:9. *The Lord knows how to deliver the godly out of temptations and reserve the unjust unto the judgment day to be punished.*

Abracadabra, I never meant to let you down; you're like a dream tree, and for you, I'll never be the man you would like me to be; with God on our side, nothing is impossible. I get the homesick blues once in a while, and I say to others, if you see Annie, please say hello. I never meant to let you down while praying to God, and God picked me up in his child lying in his hands; well, it's incredible, not being alone although there will be a real hard rain falling and soon. The miracle's like walking in my sleep or on very thin ice. Although the tide is turning in every stranger's eyes, it only takes a little perfect sense of what God wants.

2 Peter:22. *But it is happened unto them according to the true proverb. The dog has turned to his own vomit again; and the sow that was washed to her wallowing in the mire.*

To remain forever young and not to be infatuated with young lust or a groovy kind of love. Sometimes I feel I have too much information, and it causes trouble in my mind. And you have raised me, never made me feel lost, always made me feel like I belong to you like you are terrific, Grace. Although I'm the same old me, a tornado and a sense of humor and I cannot even feel that last kiss or the first kiss.

Just please come back in one piece, and I pray for your safety and protection. When I was stuck on you in the little lies, there was a time to out of sight more than I can say. And I still miss you. And I cannot fight that feeling. All I kept hearing from you was show me the money. And after the gold rush was over and I can't dance, I say to myself, sometimes is there anybody out there?

A cold, cold heart, I am not used to this type of love. That makes me lonesome that I never will feel the hug of your arms with one another. And being with someone else against me, especially being a man, that first cut is intense. It makes me comfortably numb, just like an elusive dream.

Well, I better get busy and keep in mind love is free, and all I want to do is my calling for God through the television series. I will keep you updated. I'm just tired of going up and down back- and-forth. Idaho will always be here, and I'm still behind the eight ball with God, although my intentions are not to be alone until the end. And God knows this prayer.

Sometimes. On love, and it's only make-believe like getting lost in a deep dark forest. And your friend is a sweet-talking guy, and they call him the breeze. I'm proud of you to be friendly yourself because you're worth it, and if you pray for me, I will pray for you, okay?

We went through our trials and tribulations and dance with the devil. There are two things for certain guaranteed. We are going to die. We are going to stand at the judgment seat in front of Jesus Christ, our Lord. God's gift to us is life; what we do with his life is our gift to God. We walked right through the middle of hell. And God protected us and brought us together. That in absolute self-miraculous beyond comprehension or imagination is only a love that could come from God.

Through the church, believers are taught to obey the Lord and testify concerning their Faith in Christ as Savior and honor Him by holy living. We believe in the great commission as a primary mission of the church. All believers should witness, by word and Faith, to the truths of God's word. The gospel of the Grace of God is to be preached to all the world.

Tears in the rain are equivalent to is only make-believe. Little bits and pieces that's all I receive from your life, nothing compared to the mountain of the Lord. You are my angel was such an amazing grace sharing you seemed impossible it was like you are right outside my window. Every day I've been cheated on, and I don't know how to say goodbye; all I want to do is have a heart of truth and honesty. The one-track mind of dreamboat Annie accumulates financial stability, and I tried to herd although I kept searching and praying. Every day my heartbeat and prayed to God, when will I be loved. And the dreams will be dreams, and she was my friend flying free, and she was the great imposter.

She had rhythm counting the tears flying free yet running scared. She had a cold, cold heart and pretended to be stuck on me. Annie had no intentions of going well with me, and peace will come because I will not go there again. I wanted her love, and I keep repeating it while sleeping, tossing, and turning. Brown night gorgeous girl pretended to help me make it through the night, and she changes my heart. I felt like I was on fire and wanted to drown myself because I loved her in vain. Annie kept saying, welcome to my world; now that you have the homesick blues, I am the devil in disguise.

And the devil Saying do you love me? And she would say good night, my love and evil the Spirit of nature. It was never knowing when she would be home, although it would be late at night. And do you remember it was a world on a string, so please stand back and keep searching? She loved me with her smile, and I was Mr. blue. And I never had the opportunity to kiss her and dreaming as I cried. The promised land was an allusion of love with her; it was like boots of Chinese plastic. When Annie was smiling, she had Angel eyes more than I can say about myself.

The melody was unchained and evil. The promise of unrighteous love, any way you look at it, she is a sweet-talking girl pretending to be devoted to me. All she wanted was fame and fortune, saying, come on softly to me, my dream lover. I'll be darned if I do, and danged if I don't, she would just a woman in the picture. She kept saying, and you mean everything to me, baby, you're the only one. And my shoes kept walking back to her, falling in love pretending to be forever. I would run around with my heart on fire trying to make the world go away, and it was gone is hanging on the telephone.

Yes, I have seen how she looks, and she is a great pretender of some wonderful. Annie would say, you mean everything to me, and it was like falling in love forever, the only rhythm in the rain.

And she would be Outward Bound running around saying to herself, and it's going to be a good night because of my hearts on fire. And it was gone feeling one step closer. I would say to myself, let me follow you down to hell. Traveling across the universe, it was amazing, Grace saying I have a crush on you.

Annie had a deceitful cheating heart like one of hell's warriors; the love was tainted, and praying to see the rain instead of being in the Ring of fire. She was a fantastic plastic lover, and believe me, I know, so people get ready, it will get more in-depth, and there is nobody out there. I know something about love since all I have is an allusion. I pray to God; she would release me. And he was the Eve of destruction in the house of the rising Sun promising wedding bells in love was tainted. I feel I have to run away from this tainted love we have shared; you have made my mind troubled, and it was a magical moment, but I had to break down a long time ago. I hate myself sometimes, and I want to die.

I keep hearing in my mind, baby, please don't hold me tight Eli is coming. I feel so lonesome tonight like the wind blowing, and it's the same old me. She does not love me tender in these warm Idaho knights; she comes a little bit closer to deceit and fraudulently shows me this pseudo-love. She kept saying, you belong to me, and it was a tragedy and a heatwave of one love with another with a bad reputation.

Please take a letter to my Annie and please let her know I will see her soon our love is like a rose. Like a diamond in the sea, she thinks I still care, and this half-bred love comes back to me like the fulsome prison blues. And I keep saying, come back when you grow up, girl, and tell it to the mountain because I didn't care for her, not wanting to share. Baking like a full, I'm better off without this black magic woman not sticking with me. And the Angels cried because she does not know me; she has only hit me with her best shot of evil. And getting her kicks off walking right back, knowing I may never love her again sincerely. I was a victim of circumstance as she put a little love in my heart; the raindrops did not stand by me.

These were lonely teardrops, and all she wanted was that mansion on the Hill, and it's sad to belong to someone who does not love. She loves making me lonesome and to follow after, and all she was is Annie in the skies as a disguise. And all I ever wanted was this burning love to come on over, and all she said was get me the computers give me the iPhones give me my vanilla cards, honey. And I had to go down by the river and pray and dream of a girl I would eventually kiss. And all I wanted to do was this Christian love from the real God and his holy Grace from heaven above. Although my unshakable Faith, I keep praying to God, is there anybody out there?

It just comes naturally the desire to pray and believe with Faith and love for God. And he has another man in her life with no respect, and I finally got the message that she has given to me. They say the practice is perfect, and when you feel the earth move, you can see the ice break, so please stay a while after the fire is gone and watched the great pretender be the love child. You would have thought our love was like a bed of roses and realizing it was a bed of thorns. I am a highwayman, and it feels mighty high to search out and find his girl, Annie.

I will find you when I dream of teaching you not to use my love and truly love somebody because I'm a soul man, a child of God. You made me fall to pieces, and they say that only fools fall in love, although the truth is fools rush in. Every breath she takes is a paper cut that cuts deep and hurts. Her passion was most certainly obscured by a cloudy love of sound and vision. You cannot even see the story in her eyes; she should have been me to find out what love features.

Time after time, she was cruel, like a firefly not says touch my body, and she has to be Santa Claus, my dream lover. Now that Annie is a con and nothing is left of her, she tries to crawl back what is left of her. I was crawling down and dirty Boulevard with an invisible touch of the dirty dance with the devil, and she has not got anybody. My love is alive, and it's like the heat of the night, and every woman in the world experiences love. God willing, I pray for all of my life. I had this vision of love, thank you, God.

Knowing my girl Annie was like walking on eggshells, and you had to take it easy; she was absolutely a dark Angel and not my best friend. Now my God-given guardian angel is understanding and charming, and only God had known before we were born; she is so beautiful and has a precious heart. All I can say is to my evil any as I was a fool for her and a dreamer if only I had known I would have taken it on the run it was like a dead man walking all the changes and inconsistency was like being in the rain and a night fever that never ended.

She was born to lose all the changes and so crazy I had to throw my hands up. All and he said was give me, give me without providing anything in return take as inferno one of the devil's helpers. God knows I do not have to take any more chances with unshakable faith prayers and love for God. I do not have to be flogged anymore and absolutely no more lies because Annie is going down with her gigolo. Traders never play hangman; it's always a crazy world, and eventually, you break down what they do not know is they are going down like lady blue, her gigolo, and she is all out of time.

Annie and her gigolo are broken, going their way as if anyone cared; these souls are haunted and processed will never survive. I respect you, and I cherish our friendship. I want you to know that you are in my thoughts and prayers during this crucial time in our lives. I'm proud of you, and You are an amazing soul far ahead of your time. An old soul. Who has taught this God-fearing child of God, and brought me this for the reason of the pure religion.

You'll never even have the thought of taking me home tonight for the first and last kiss I have never received. And then you have to question your childhood and could have been a crazy world and made you a lonely girl. You call me baby, and it's only my dream of a girl dancing 8 miles high. Next to you is sitting your gigolo; what a glamorous life. You will be just another brick in the wall if anyone at all cares about your black sexy love. Although that's your thing, John is not far away from my girl Annie and her gigolo.

So go your own way; we are broken, never to be heroes in the eyes of God. You always look beautiful, you know I both know your heart is black, and she ends up a lonely girl, not only an evil black heart but a wrinkled soul. A cold heart I miss the falling snow is a life you will always know. Little moments with your gigolo are lusting after the world amongst beautiful people knowing you are neither hot nor cold. You are lost in the world fighting fire with fire and evil black heart that only time of the life haunted and you have not seen anything yet. Annie and her gigolo can tell the angels in heaven they have never seen evil so personified as they have of the evil they have done.

A soul lost is never anything there for my God. And it's not my imagination experiencing this evil forever down would make a man cry. The thoughts of giving me back my bullets and do not look down because I will never be alone through the Grace of God. You have loved me sexy and your evil talking head adventures forward into a fraudulent lifestyle of chasing the lust of money. Without being seen behind your computer screen is the cowardly soul you are with your gigolo.

I have never read in the Bible where to pray or forgive the devil. I have no prayers if you forget you and do not let you or your gigolo rent space in my head and turn it over to God. You are a predator with your gigolo; this is Annie; she will bring you forever down. I'm never alone with the Holy Spirit working through me to help many other souls to the gates of heaven; this I pray God willing. There was a time when you made me feel you are the air beneath my wings, and I had the lovesick blues. You have never tried; there is no real hope because you and your gigolo are gone, and you will do it again because you are in unchained Melody. I'm not with you.

I had to love the gift of forgetting about you; that was the greatest gift of all. I'm just a ghost in your house, and here I am with a girl Annie from the North country. I will find someone you're not the boss or the big shot anymore with your gigolo. I cannot help but think about your mother if you ever have one or had one that you proclaim to be taking care of; every word I find from your mouth is a lie, I find simply unbelievable.

When I think about you, I can't help but wonder if there's any salvation for your soul along with your gigolo friend; it will be next to nothing gratefully dead because you feel you are a sophisticated lady and you are strong enough. Hell is for real, and you will burn like a rocket for a short time proclaiming your narcissistic personality to those precious poor souls children of God that you have deceived fraudulently with your gigolo.

The life you have never shared with me feels like you and your gigolo taking advantage of others in your fraudulent evil characteristics. And in your heart, do you want to touch me? Well, don't touch me because you are a creep that says show me the money. And all you say is I want you to want me, and you are such a dirty laundry bag with your gigolo. I do not want to be loved like that. I breathe in, breath out, and Annie and her gigolo are not okay; God is watching, and God knows. If you like, you are celebrities with your cold, cold hearts dancing through the day, bringing the big noise of the gold rush bruising many others hungry for you.

You are a song for someone, and you cut deep grooves into those souls, and all my friends say it will not be long before you are homeless, and there will be no bright side of the road. So I had to touch myself and search my soul, finding out that love hurts. Waiting on a woman as you stuck in the middle with you and your gigolo feels like I have been deceived like dust in the wind as a wanderer I did not know.

I'm curious to know of your mother's depression; your mother must know and not be proud of you or your father, especially having a gigolo control your life and your slipping and sliding away. You and your gigolo are better together; you find out that it is a groovy kind of greed. I'm moving on, and like Sodom and Gomorrah, Annie and her gigolo will be like fire and ice. I have to go my own way or another, and you have never even thought about touching my body or wanting to be next to each other.

Like Christmas morning, sad but true you never believed in Santa Claus or miracles. Only God knows the way, and you are like the devil with boots of Chinese plastic. What's left of me? Thank God for my unshakable Faith, and I am nice to myself because I am worth it. I will never go crawling back to Annie and her gigolo because the glitter has faded. She is like a dirty Boulevard invisible to touch and does her dirty dancing with the devil, and the devil gives it to her controls her with her gigolo.

Dirty dancing with the devil they carry on, so beware when you go online and look at those beautiful pictures of these ladies that are the devil in disguise. And every word from their mouth is a lie; they are cheap tricks like mud on the tires. I have not got anybody yet, but my love is alive, and like the heat of the night, I have the vision and a prayer for love.

I had visions of love; only the Lord knew I was walking on eggshells, so I had to take it easy. I believed in this pseudo-love that this angel and Annie were born to lose with her young lust. And I thought she was my best friend, though I would stay in love found out it was a Mexican blues. I had dreams of this French Canadian lady being an All-American girl. With my night fever, I've underestimated my charming beauty.

I was a fool for her and a dreamer I had to break down, and I never knew I had to take it on the run and tell her she was beautiful. I asked her to dream a little dream of me, and it was a wild night. The more boys she met, I was a dead man walking with changes, and I have never seen the rain. I want so crazy I throw my hands. The chances I had taken her and her gigolo were under my skin. This girl Annie and her gigolo or the Queen and King of the Stone Age. Great is the faithfulness.

I had to come and get her love, and she would say, next, contestant, and please, I'm busy. How many other men were paying money listening to this Angel face being coerced and manipulated? They were flogging many. And the amazing Grace was out of time; there were no more lies. That's where it is when she cries. I pray to God her gigolo will be there. I do not know much, although going down, she did not light up my life because our love was not so right. I had to break down crystal tears and isn't it funny she would not take me home tonight.

The last kiss belongs to her gigolo. Eventually, I will say, hey, there lonely girl. Have you forgotten about the Grace of God, our Faith, our prayers, and our love for God? Annie and her gigolo were traders, and they should never play hangman. She took others with her glamorous life next to you sitting next to me about this girl Annie. It was a sexy love, and it was her thing; never far away, she always was thinking, go your own way; we are broken. Annie would say, you're not my hero, as she would say, too many others with her flawed thinking and her gigolo laughing.

There was a time when she was beautiful tonight, and you and I both know there were little moments like that that imagined that she wanted to be a beautiful soul. But she was hot and cold with her gigolo. A haunted life of paranoia with no conscience and no soul, only in time I will survive not fighting fire with fire although lost in thought. Annie's gigolo has always overjoyed another sucker to remember. Oh my God is just my imagination, although this man child of God can cry and never go down.

I do not want to look down and never be alone; I do not love this sexy woman who only has the lovesick blues. Some hearts were like wind beneath my wings, of course, and he does not cry anymore because I am gone, she hopes. With another brick in the wall is all these poor souls mean to Annie and her gigolo. And I say what about love, and it has to be the greatest gift of all. I have been cured; I will never do it again unchained from this evil melody when I'm without her, there will never be another—taking advantage of a man.

Annie and her gigolo do not care, they will always be chasing their tail, and only the chaos and turmoil I cannot even imagine. Neither Annie nor her gigolo will ever do it again because I will be without her. And I ask myself, what about love? The greatest gift of all, I feel like I'm just a ghost. So please, beware of the girl named Annie and her gigolo because they do not care. The devil owns their soul, and evil is so personified even the angels in heaven do not care. Because these are a pair will only know despair, grief turmoil within their greed, they will always be in desperate need.

Here I am in the French Canadian girl from the North country has taught me a lot over the time she has taken advantage of my love. Annie and her gigolo have not only taken advantage of me but others as well, acting like the big shot and nobody can do better because they think they are the boss. God is watching, and God knows all; they will be judged on their thoughts on their words, what they do, and what they fail to do.

They will burn in hell next to nothing, although the sophisticated lady is strong enough at present, and she does not want anyone to touch her. The cowardly soul only knows words and pictures on the Internet that draws many into her web of lies. And saying show me the money honey or give me the computers or iPhones. And she says to others, and I want you to want me because I'm beautiful. I have no dirty laundry in this house. I want you to love me like that so I can breathe in, and you can breathe out.

And only God knows of these cold, cold hearts thinking they are dancing in the days bringing the noise after the gold rush they will be bruised. And hungry for the love they have never known, it will be a song for someone. All my friends say Annie and her gigolo will be homeless without a place or face or a soul and never seeing the bright side of the road. I love myself because I'm worth it. I'm proud of myself and my life because Jesus Christ, our Lord, has taken the wheel.

And Annie is a wild child saying, isn't it romantic although there's something about you if I didn't know any better diamonds aren't forever. Annie and her gigolo are addicted like they are on a train for Auschwitz. Their dreams are a Mockingbird, and I do not care to be in love with evil intent. Annie always says girls want to have fun, although don't get me wrong, I can see it in her eyes. There were clouds in my soul, and I was on the run. I wanted to be starting something of Christian love in this deep majestic forest where the Holy Spirit lives, although I'm only a country boy born in the mountains.

Annie and her gigolo are about all out of time, and there will be no son, no intimate truth; they are wasting time and going down to the depths of hell where the road is wide and paved with good intentions. Blinded by evil and a life of lies and deceit, they know spiritual discernment; that's why God has given us a conscience. The light blinds them, and the gigolo and Annie stay in the dark guilty of society. Remember that there are many Annie's and gigolo's out there to take light, deceive and steal and try to take your soul. And Annie keeps saying, you're all I have and thinking to herself she will always be unfaithful because of a dream shield she has ongoing back-and-forth teardrops never fall.

Although she can turn it on again and again, saying, baby, it's cold outside. And asking you where you are going and once again getting caught in the web of lies that are so big you will feel like jumping into the ocean. And you will learn not to cherish honesty or trust because Annie and her gigolo will always have and always will hold on. Saying you belong to me to shake it off the reason is in your heart it's you and me baby and is the fight of the song of the slipknot around your neck. So we do not have to die to live to the Grace of God; if we keep our Faith, say our prayers, and have our love for God, we will never sleep alone.

Like John, the Revelator and the prophecy will light the way. And cast every other one into the fire wishing they were not there begging for one drop of water and praying to God to let them die, and God will not give them one drop of water or let them die. So I say goodbye to this evil Annie and her so-called friend, the gigolo; it's been a long journey. And baby, you're no longer my destiny; you're like the Blue Bayou, and I do not want you back or will I cry for you. The way she looked at one time in the night brought me happiness, and I wanted to come over and be together, the promises I had heard.

And did not know everything about her; she was a fallen Angel. God, my father in heaven, I prayed as I cried, trying to live my life of a love story, and I found myself once again dancing with the devil. And I said to Annie, and I do not have time for this pain; you have too much pride, and your gigolo is so proud. And I would say to Annie as I tried to shine the light and sure the way come and follow me through our trials and tribulations on this golden road to heaven, and there were times we were feeling good. And I found out she was wearing her sunglasses at night saying, take me as I am, and you can have me. Come to my window because I miss you and we would break up to make up.

We had secrets, emptied my soul to her, and shared my life, and she never shared her life with me; she always had secrets. So if you run across Annie and her gigolo, make sure that they share their life with you every detail that is the key to understanding these evil unfaithful tricks that they can make you believe. Drift away from these evil souls even if they cry like a baby, just like the girl named Annie keep her far away and do not believe one word she says. She is very similar to a man trying to get into a lady's pants. This man will tell a lady anything that he thinks she wants to hear so that he can get into her pants.

Annie has always mentioned how she was sitting in the care of her mother. I was sick her mother was and dragging her mother around from Calgary, Canada, to Montréal Canada two Malta, a small island off Italy. And taking her mother to Brussels, and her mother was in Uganda, Africa. And for her mother being so sick all the time and depressed, her mother sure enjoys traveling. Always the excuse of taking care of her mother her taking her to the hospital. She kept herself far away, very seldom calling on the telephone. Please do not believe this Northern chicken from

Canada and her gigolo with her so-called mother that I do not believe in telling you the truth.

I finally did it my way. I cannot live that lie anymore; the gravity of love was falling, and I was saying God, I am alive. And God answered my prayers when I had hit my bottom with the most beautiful miracle of understanding and not falling for this black angel with the black heart with an evil gigolo in the background. Her soul is similar to dishes of dirt, saying you are my all in all. I am remodeling an old shack into a stunning home, spending a lot of time and money doing so. I have to thank Annie and her gigolo for this beautiful home in this manuscript I am writing so others may know do not believe one word on the Internet. Unless they call you on the telephone and talk with you or video chat face-to- face, they never ask you for money. Arrange a meeting as soon as possible and stick close to home. Or she will be knocking on your door in your head, saying, do I ever cross your mind?

In all, she is a black beauty with a black heart and a black soul. The devil in disguise trying to get your soul, and there is no beauty in this dance. So I find myself better off alone, and God will deliver me all the way home with my unshakable Faith even though I can't dance. Time after time, I pray as a man who can be moved by the Holy Spirit. By the way, Annie and her gigolo, you will never know their real names, and they will make phony passports to make you believe their lies. Keep in mind Satan is the father of all liars, and they have their place in hell. So don't stand too close to them because they may not be coming home tonight. We all have our trials and tribulations go through, and we have the spiritual gifts we have our character defects.

The answer is to keep growing along spiritual lines praying to God and thanking God daily, and doing the right thing in this world can be as in the Lord's prayer, "on earth as it is in heaven." Annie will always tell you have I told you lately that I love you and sing this song for the lonely grand illusion saying I miss you. Say goodbye immediately whenever you're asked for funds or money. That is the bottom line from a cold, cold heart; she can't love you, so give it up immediately. In this world, they will be all out of love eventually, and they will all die young, and we need a resolution for these romantic scammers. You say, how do I live? I'll never leave them alone for one good reason; it may be by calling to expose their fantasy of them saying, I'm so lost without you just one more time. Space between there should be short; otherwise, your love Will lead to madness.

As they say, Give me more, and they will bring down the house. And it will be a lonely night, and you will say how deep is my love for this woman who wants to be rich. She is crazy, and she is beautiful, although very cunning powerful, and baffling. It was like the wolves raised her. Going after the easy money and wanting you to be loved by her. She will say, don't make me wait for love as the dove cries, making you think she is forever young, slipping a silver dagger into your inside. Saying this is one for my baby, let the bleeding strike I will be best friends.

It will be drums of thunder right now, and she will strip you of your flesh with the midnight motion, and I will start saying goodbye with her sad-eyed words. She is a lowlife who will damage you like drowning in the river with brain damage. She will always be in a place where you will not be able to drive all night long, claiming to be best friends, although Annie's secret it is a little liar and is the devil stance with her gigolo. And you will think to yourself, and just when I needed her most, she will always let you down; don't fall for her black heart. Like shooting stars and shadows, Annie and her gigolo have burnout quickly in the night as a distant deceiving friend who lurks in the dark shadows like a coward.

Annie is nothing but a cheap trick is broken down places, and you think you got it bad. Annie and her gigolo are always on the move, so they are tough to catch like they are blowing in the wind trying to get chimes of freedom. And paranoid that they will be taught they are always free-falling, never with a solid foundation. They are tough lessons learned, and they are just waiting for worms. Getting nearer to the prison and confinement, so always stop believing and take them down. Someone like you Will catches this lady, and her gigolo does not let them slide or fly. They are doing it too many, hundreds of thousands of others.

It's called hot tub Christianity; if it feels good, do it. Annie and her gigolo are facing immortality and eternity in a place called hell or Hades. They will not be able to breathe; they will be drinking fusion juice choose and thinking back just when I needed this man most, I took advantage of him, and they're going to hell to chill. There are different levels of hell, as in Dante's towering inferno. The lowest level of hell is called Tartarus. You are frozen under ice, not able to see either half out of the ice or half under the ice are under the ice for eternity, and this is the place for treachery and traders.

This is the place where you will find Annie and her gigolo. It's beyond frightful beyond Erie beyond evil; the feeling, from what I understand, makes you feel like you will never want to die because you will possibly go there. While Annie and her gigolo ever find themselves? Drifting in the air that I breathe, telling you, let's make love. With every breaking wave, Annie and a gigolo say all I want is you and your money. They could be a reflection of your life climbing the ladder. Sing bang, bang, and it's all over now. And you will say to yourself."

CHAPTER 3

THIS LADY GINETTE,
THE ANSWER TO MY PRAYER

THOMAS WROTE; PLEASE LET ME know if you do not want to hear any biblical verses. I walk by Faith, not by sight. You are so precious and an answer to my prayer, and I thank God for you in my life. God's gift to us is life; what we do with this life is our gift to God.

Galatians 5; 16. *This, I say then, Walk in the Spirit, and you shall not fulfill the lust of the flesh. For the flesh lust against the Spirit and the Spirit, against the flesh; these are contrary to the other, so you cannot do the things you would. But if you be led of the Spirit, you are not under the law. Now the works of the flesh are manifest, which are these; Adultery, fornication, uncleanliness, idolatry, witchcraft, hatred, variance, emulations, wrath, strife, seditions, heresies, envy, murderers, drunkenness, revealing's, and such like; of the which I tell you before, as I have also told you in time past, that they which do such things shall not inherit the kingdom of God.*[22]. *But the fruit of the Spirit is love, joy, peace, long-suffering, gentleness, goodness, Faith, meekness, temperance; against such, and there is no law.*[24]*. And they that are Christ have crucified the flesh with the affections of lusts. If we live in the Spirit, let us also walk in the Spirit. Let us not be desirous of vain glory, provoking one another, envying one another.*

Thomas wrote; This is what the Spirit leads me to do daily is the Grace of God. I pray you are keeping well. I pray for you continuously; you consume my every thought with prayer and safety that the Holy Spirit and your guardian angels will guide your soul's journey through this life.

As our spirits have come together for a very miraculous gracious meaning that is so supernatural and we can thank my father, who miraculously has the same birthday as yourself, for opening our eyes to a miracle through the Grace of God, our Faith, our prayers, and our love for God and each other. That nothing happens perchance; everything happens for a reason. And more shall be revealed between the two of us.

Praying to God and the way you came into my life miraculously, because of the gigolo and Annie opened the door and put their heads into the rope to be exposed.

And I pray to God, God willing, it will be a calling we will have together one day. I have been praying to God for the last two days to find out if Annie was real and found out she has this gigolo that controls through the Holy Spirit. You have been in answer to my prayer, and I thank God so very much for you in my life. Are you an amazing lady, you know that?

I'm proud of you, so be nice to yourself, because you are most certainly worth it. No worry, no stress, that is a moment of happiness we will never get back. I love you with reverence. God bless with love and prayers; say your prayers I will pray for you if you pray for me. Thank you, and have a good day or evening. By the way, I got a call from Annie last night; when I picked up the phone, she hung up on me. I got the call back number, and it was her. She is not sent any emails; thank God.

The gigolo and Annie from their fraudulent romantic scams. And I'm serious; we are not the only ones they are scamming. We have to work and put them away. I don't believe those are their real names; as a matter of fact, I do not believe anything they say is the truth. One thing good about Canada is romantic scammers get up to six years to 12 years in prison. We have to put them there, okay? We keep God; first, we say our prayers together, devoting our lives to God and service

The gigolo Mark tells you he is sick. The gigolo is not sick. I wish you would quit falling for the scam. I'm having my book published Friday. Now, what makes you think that God has matched you with the gigolo? Give me a break.

The devil connected you with the gigolo, and through our prayers, God turned it around in a miraculous way. A gigolo is a man whom you love, and he is not taking care of you. Think about it. Get rid of the gigolo. He does not reach you on Christmas does not let you know where he is at.

Your friend, the gigolo, and Annie are a couple together. They are professional scammers. I have already had an investigator check them out, and if I pay them a little more money, they will put them both in prison in Canada for six years or even up to 12 years. That's why they are moving all the time on the run. And God put you and the gigolo together.? I believe that that the gigolo is lying to you, saying that he is sick. So he can make love to Annie. You just don't get it. God bless with love and prayers.

Thomas wrote; I pray you are keeping well; the only reason you are sick is the gigolo. Do you say he is your fiancé? Where does he live? How far do you live apart from him? And the only reason he comes to see you in so he can get into your pants. And he's taken money from you, and I should say you gave it to him because you think he loves you. And he says he has a construction company in Africa? Give me a break. He is a liar is a con artist. Do not believe one word of what he says. I went through the same thing with Annie. And you said that Annie was the gigolo's step-father, making Dorris, Annie's mother, Mark's husband. I'll tell you what's happening: the gigolo and Annie are con artists, and Annie does not have any sick mother. It's all a lie and a scam.

Using a sick mother is a great way to get money. And I'm sure he loves you physically to where you have fallen in love with him. And you give him money because you think he loves you. Annie has written to me long, long emails every day. I am sure he is superior to you when he knows you have money to give him. And he treats you extra lovely to get that money. And he tells you he loves you, and you're going to have maids and butlers in a big house and servants and cooks. Give me a break. The sooner you dump him, the better off you will feel.

Knowing you feel that way about this con artist, this gigolo is all he is a gigolo; he lives up to lady's money. He does not work for a living; he never has. You are just gullible. The gigolo uses his sickness as an excuse not to work because he is a sluggard. In the Bible, a sluggard is so lazy when they lift their spoon to their mouth from the soup bowl; they fall in the soup bowl and drown. Now that's lazy, and that's what the gigolo is, and Annie is just as lazy. They are professional scammers and con artists. They are in bed together.

The beautiful pictures and the lovely emails and talking about God. Thomas, is the only one talking about God. And Annie was like a man trying to get into a lady's pants. She never shared her life with me at all. She just replied to everything I shared with her, and I shared everything with her. Thomas studied the Bible, and Thomas still tries to shine the flashlight in front of her to see the light. Not while you are still going with this idiot. He is illiterate is ignorant; maybe he was just born that way.

Get away from him immediately. And you will start feeling better. You would feel better if you had a man that provided for you and give you a place to live, and treated you like a queen without you having to give him anything financially. I know you would. Maybe you have to hit your bottom, and I pray to God, you are taking my advice. I'll tell you the gigolo and Annie and her so-called mother are always traveling on other people's money, and they are still in disguise, changing their looks all the time because they are scared to get caught. And that's why they move all the time they are doing very well although they are spending all that money.

And Annie uses your passport with your name and signature and passes herself off as you. I cannot help you anymore because you are still in love with the gigolo who will use you until you finally figured it out. Although when I go to the authorities, we are going to need some statements from you. This can be accomplished through emails, and I'm sure so keep a journal of times and dates when he calls what you talk about blah-blah-blah.

Do you know what the unforgivable sin is? Is blasphemy against the Holy Spirit. And you are going to hell with them. What blasphemy is, is if you know the difference between right and wrong is called spiritual discernment. And you do not say anything to the person that is doing wrong; you are committing blasphemy against the Holy Spirit. Believe me and trust me because I'm honest, I will take care of you, and you will feel 100% better. If you do not adhere to this advice that the Holy Spirit working through me is giving you, I cannot help you. God bless with love and prayers.

Do not be mistaken through a beautiful picture of a lady who will entice a man to give her money fraudulently. Through lying continuously in telling this man exactly what he wants to hear. She lives by lust, and that is taking. If she lived by love, she would be giving. But she does not provide one thing; she takes.

Annie the, Romantic scammers are making a good living through deceit and fraudulent lying continuously and false promises. Most of these ladies are controlled by a gigolo (a man who makes his living by using a lady or young girl). Somehow these scammers of romance can get and purchase iPhones and computers from the United States have them mailed to New York and then on to wherever they are for resale. Using other people's Social Security numbers and various vanilla cards iTunes cards, all they need is someone like a sucker to get them and mail them to them where they will resell wherever they are and make money illegally.

Yes, the last address you used to send the package was approximately ten other addresses, always changing places, never in the same place at the same time, very elusive living in the dark. One thing Annie and her gigolo cannot do is lie. You can always remember the truth, but you can never remember a lie. And the devil is the father of liars, and their souls will be doomed to hell for eternity, in a place that has no windows, has no doors, and is so evil and eerie beyond the comprehension or imagination.

This address immediately below is Annie's uncle Daniel in Malta, where she went to stay for one year with her mother. And God only knows they may have not even left Canada, wherever they are. Online romantic scammers can take on a whole deceitful names, addresses, locations; they have all the right pictures and can draw in innocent man into their web of lies and thievery where you will find in the end the depths of their souls for eternity will remain infinity. For a reason, they have no fear or no belief in Jesus Christ our Lord or God who sent his only Son into this world. When Jesus Christ our Lord ascended into heaven, he left us with the Holy Spirit that moves throughout the earth, answering prayers and through others to help one another.

Another trick of these romance scammers is finding out through Annie where her so-called pseudo-fiancé lives. The gigolos are usually more than one, can break into the homes of the unsuspecting man who feels he has fallen in love with the love of his life. These gigolos can fraudulently take identities such as driver's license, Social Security cards, and even military identification cards and make copies of them, removing them from the home of the unsuspected man. He thought he was in love with Annie.

Thomas had no idea that his identification was stolen from his home and used fraudulently to make purchases and deceive patrons of businesses by using these identification cards that have been stolen from an innocent man like Thomas. And Thomas could be held liable for the fraudulent use of his identification cards. Beware of these gigolo's and their Annie's. They are out there waiting for an unsuspecting man who is about to fall in love with the devil and the Sons of perdition. Surprises will come and on it's way.

AUTHORITIES AND HELL.

CHAPTER 4

THIS IS GINETTE;
I PRAY FOR AN EQUALLY YOKED
CHRISTIAN SOULMATE

THOMAS MET THROUGH PRAYER IN such a miraculous way through the Grace of God; it defies the imagination, and only God knows the address below. I sent her the passport, and she said that was her signature on the passport, but the passport picture was not Ginette's picture. What is miraculous is that you are both French-Canadian, and I love the French Canadian accent. You're not only an answer to my prayer; only God knows you could be my real soulmate.

Thomas wrote; Ginette, you are like a guardian angel. I pray for you for the last two days with Faith and love for God; you're a miracle and an answer. Annie sent me a passport with Ginette's signature on it – the 22nd of July 2019 –.And I'm assuming you have a photo ID when identification with your picture on it; I know you must have a passport. And there is nothing personal on that that I should not take a look at, especially your friend.? I would like to see a picture of you with your photo ID if you would be so kind.

Thomas found himself praying and praying to God, saying, please, God help me find out if this girl Annie is for real or is you fraudulent and deceitful? It did not take Thomas but two days unbeknownst to him. The only time Thomas has sent money to his fiancée, Annie $100 one day through PayPal and came to find out, and she did not have a PayPal account. So Annie used what she claimed to be a friend of her statement. And was the same name and a different email address, only having her last name and her first initial. Thomas thought it was on the up and up. Annie and her fiancé seem to be on the up and up until she was not contacting him, so Thomas thought he would send an email to the email account on PayPal and three other emails that Annie has. The prayers paid off, and a miracle happened.

A different lady responded to Thomas, and she mentioned not to send any more emails to Annie because she was a fraud. Thomas was a little shocked; this lady even gave Thomas her telephone number. And her first name is Ginette. So Thomas called her instantly when she gave him her telephone number. She sounded very charming, and if you can believe this or not, God has a strange way. Ginette's fiancé was not calling her on the telephone and was taking money from her, and she wanted to know if Thomas would contact him on Christmas to wish him a Merry Christmas.

After talking for some time, Thomas found out that Annie was with a gigolo named Mark. And Mark was Annie's lover. And it was Ginette's fiancé. It was getting confusing so hang on for this ride. It seems Ginette's fiancé, Mark had taken or stolen Ginette's passport. Then he gave it to his friend Annie and somehow, the gigolo Mark had taken Annie's picture and somehow patched it on to Ginette's passport. And then the gigolo gave the passport to Annie to use fraudulently. Without Ginette's knowledge.

Thomas and Ginette talked daily to get to know one another and find out what Annie and her gigolo Mark were doing. And only God knows their real names. It seems Annie's gigolo Mark swindled Ginette out of $8000. And love has a strange way. Ginette was madly in love with Mark even after this gigolo ripped her off and would not call her or let Ginette know where he was staying. Thomas instantly picked up on it and said, are you serious? Mark and Annie are in bed together. And Ginette, you are what I have been praying for to God. You are a miracle.

The money Thomas sent to Annie was from Ginette's PayPal account. And Annie used Ginette's passport, which Ginette's signature, although the passport was not Ginette's picture. What a mess; it even gives Thomas a headache writing about this. Ginette is such a sweetheart, and she has never lied to Thomas, and she said first things that she would never lie to Thomas. So day after day, Thomas talked on the telephone and sent each other emails. Although Thomas cannot convince Ginette that her fiancé, gigolo, is taking advantage of her, she is that much in love with him. Although Thomas continues chipping away a little at a time, Ginette finally starts to see the light. Thomas and Ginette are also Christians equally yoked spiritually. They have more in common than they ever thought they had. They are falling in love with each other. The gigolo and Annie are French-Canadian as well as Ginette. Thomas is skeptical and in a state of disbelief, thinking this is another con job, and it very well could be. However, Ginette sounds so sincere and wants to meet Thomas as soon as possible in Idaho. Although because of this, coronavirus has the whole world and locked down.

As soon as they get the opportunity, they plan on coming together. Thomas let Ginette know that he will not fornicate; he is a Christian and loves God, and wants to do it right this time. The exchange seems to agree. Sex outside of marriage is a sin and abomination against God.

CHAPTER 5

THOMAS HAS FOUND A BRAND-NEW LOVE MIRACULOUSLY, AND GINETTE LOVES THOMAS.

AND AS THIS SERIES MOVES forward, there will be more twists and turns than a pet gofer burrowing throughout his hole, and hang on, see if you can see which way these critters are going. It is fascinating. And love is unbelievable. The love that Thomas has for God surpasses the imagination or comprehension. Thomas looks at these souls as lost as he understood that Annie was lying quite a while ago and tried to shine the light so this one lost sheep could find her way. Although greed is a very cunning powerful baffling way, Satan, Thomas is afraid, has got her soul for eternity going to hell. That's unfortunate. Sometimes Thomas wonders and just curious why certain people do not have a conscience to decipher the difference between right and wrong and take advantage of others. That's when Thomas finds himself praying and praying hard to God, and that's when the miracles happen, such as his new beautiful lady Ginette. Although hang on for the ride. Smile.

Thomas reaches out to the pornography industry. Thomas is mainly trying to get married men sitting at home, sending these ladies money, thinking that they will get married one day, and live happily ever after. Thomas is thinking, give me a break, please. Not one place in the Bible does God say to pray for Satan or forgive him. Thomas is tired of being a doormat. Thomas has three questions he always asked ladies online, how much money do you have? How old are you? Ladies still lie about that. And how much you weigh? Smile, and ladies indeed lie about that one. Using makes the conversations brief; although impressive, Thomas does have a great sense of humor and loves to laugh; it keeps him young. Thomas has no regrets or resentments. That is a moment of happiness he will never get back. Insist on enjoying life, Thomas refuses to have one negative moment. And does not take himself too seriously. Stay in the moment; the last minute is gone, the next minute is not here yet, right at this very moment, everything is okay. Okay? It takes practice, although it can be accomplished through the Grace of God.

Thomas loves Ginette so much, and she is planning a trip to Idaho state very soon; they are talking about it and even talking about living together. However, Thomas and Ginette are focused on putting Annie and her gigolo away in the Canadian prison, not to do their escapades with others. And destroy other marriages and relationships through romantic fraudulent evil love.

My guardian angel treasure is excellent in thy faithfulness and says, come and get my love; she has the heart of an angel, and that's where it is. When she cries, I want to be there to light up your life because our love is so right. Isn't it funny how time slips away, and my guardian angel treasure is going to take me home tonight no more lonely girl? My guardian angel treasure as a Queen and takes me with a glamorous life. And if only everyone cared as we do with our sexy love because it's our thing never far away; she is my hero and wonderful tonight, and it's little moments like that that make her beautiful for the brevity of time only a twinkle, God has given his holy Grace.

1 Corinthians 7;2. *Nevertheless, to avoid fornication, let every man have his wife, and let every woman have her husband.*

2 Corinthians 6;14. *Be ye not unequally yoked together with unbelievers: for what fellowship hath righteousness with unrighteousness? and what communion hath light with darkness? The wife does not have authority over her own body, but the husband does. And likewise, the husband does not have authority over his own body, but the wife does.*

Ecclesiastes 4; 10. *– For if they fall, the one will lift his fellow; but woe to him that is alone when he falls; for he has not another to help him up.*

Ecclesiastes 4; 11 *– Again, If to lie together, they have heat; but how can one be warm alone?*

Psalms 91; 11. *For he shall give his angels charge over thee, to keep thee in all thy ways.*

Ephesians 5; 6-8. *Let no man deceive you with vain words, for because of these things comes the wrath of God upon the children of disobedience. Be not you, therefore, partakers with them. For you were sometimes darkness, but now are you light in the Lord; walk as children of light.*

Ginette has her passport, although how it was taken from her is another scammer's gigolo of gigolo's the coward of cowards. The gigolo will romantically get involved (Mark) with an unsuspecting lady and promise the world while at the same time stealing her identification cards. And then passing them on to Annie. For this reason, it takes an evil woman to be deceitful to an innocent lady who thinks she has fallen in love with the man of her dreams. A man cannot use a lady's identification and vice versa for fraudulent scams.

I will put Mark (the gigolo) at the place that he goes to jail.

Don't send Annie anything anymore; Mark, the gigolo control Annie.

Do not tell her that you know me! Because I'll make Mark (the gigolo) go to jail. Don't tell anyone that we have to talk. Very important!!!!

I NEVER LIE, but this day I lied to Morris, another gigolo, who just happened to be married to Annie's mother for a short time until Annie and her mother were suspicious of Morris and discarded him from their lives. However, used Morris later on down the road and broke him in as another gigolo. Can anyone even imagine the deceit and fraudulent stealing and lying between these gigolos and their deceitful ladies? It must be constant turmoil and chaos. If you do good things, good things happen if you do bad things, bad things happen, and it's that simple. Although these ignorant, illiterate brain-dead team of the devil's disciples have no souls or any conscience.

Ginette stated, "Because I knew that he was stealing money from Mark. I told him that if he wanted to be free better work with Mark. That case is closed but give me the info.

Hey, I will send you a picture. Can you send me a bible in french!! I have a gift since I, two years old I have a suspicion. I feel the Spirit in a room. All subjects I can feel right and wrong kind of person. Yesterday Mark said he would kill me if I am unfaithful. He means it! So if you can help me with the most Infos that, I can put him behind bars. Thank you. Yours sincerely, Ginette.

Thomas wrote; no worry, no stress the gigolo Mark is a coward and one of Satan's helpers through fear and intimidation, especially to ladies. Gigolo would never face a man with courage. Gigolo and Annie hide behind computers and words, and they fear the daylight because they are the devil's helpers (perdition).

So, Thomas is excited about putting Annie away with her gigolo, the fiancé to Ginette. Ginette and Thomas are working together to put Annie and her gigolo Mark behind bars; this should not continue, and it will if the not stop.

CHAPTER 6

JANESSA A REAL LOVING-KINDNESS, UNFORTUNATELY, HER PICTURES USED BY SCAMMERS

THOMAS HAS RESEARCHED SO MANY online dating scams, like the picture Annie was using was this beautiful model from Brazil who 86 romance scammers are using her photos.

Thomas finally talked of her video-chatted lovely lady and said she is finished with the business. Although she still does, Thomas assumes video chatting, whatever they call that. However, she's out of the industry of pornography. And seem to be down-to- earth and honest. After video chatting and seeing her in person finally, Thomas has found the real Annie. And she most certainly is not from Canada. She is from Brazil speaks excellent English. And said that she was tired of the FBI continuously investigating her because of all of these scammers using her pictures.

Thomas was catching on because Annie was lying continuously with her immaturity and sometimes not knowing which man she was writing to.

Thomas picked it up and started doing a little investigating and just about contacting all of these 86 romantic scammers proclaim Janessa (these pictures Annie is using).

Thomas able to finally contact the real Janessa. From Tampa, Florida. "Janessa called him on the telephone after Thomas was persistent in sending Janessa emails." Janessa is a sweetheart; she answered all of Thomas's questions and called Thomas on several occasions to see how things were going. Janessa had mentioned to Thomas, "The FBI has investigated her so many times from these fraudulent scammers using her pictures. Janessa will do anything to help catch these scammers. A real beautiful lady not only one of God's creations from the outside but her heart is just as beautiful.

Thomas right away that this lady could be a guardian angel for any man who would treat her with respect, care, and love. And Janessa will open about her modeling and some pornography shots. And will disclose her information to anyone, including the authorities, as she has done numerous times before, although Janessa is getting tired of these scammers. Thomas was proud to have met her called Thomas; Thomas was heartbroken and could not believe that his girl Annie proclaimed Janessa. Janessa picked up on Thomas is feeling and call him right away on the telephone.

CHAPTER 7

AN ANONYMOUS LADY
SENT THIS NOTE TO THOMAS

DON'T FALL TO JANESSA (**ANNIE**); my husband was a scam by her, big time!!!! It's just a picture, but not those people you are talking to or texting are not real from Nigeria; they will ask you a lot of money by giving you many excuses. My husband broke my heart, and I'm still dealing with it. He stopped, but my trust not the same. The profile is 1000 fake, and once you are into her, you will tough time getting out!!!! Because of your falling in love! They frequently change their names, but you're texting to the same scammer.

Printed in the United States
By Bookmasters